5–7–5

The Haiku of Basho

The Buddhist Society Trust is a distinguished press
in the United Kingdom which enriches lives around the
world by advancing the study and practice of Buddhism.

Its activities are supported by charitable contributions
from individuals and institutions.

For more information visit: info@thebuddhistsociety.org

First published by The Buddhist Society Trust, 2019
© Professor John White and Reverend Kemmyo Taira Sato

The Buddhist Society Trust
E: middlewayandpublishing@gmail.com

ISBN: 978-0-901032-54-6
(The Buddhist Society Trust)

A catalogue record for this book is available
from the British Library

Edited by Sarah Auld
Designed by Avni Patel

Printed and bound in Wales by Gomer Press

5 – 7 – 5

The Haiku of Basho

John White & Kemmyo Taira Sato

THE BUDDHIST SOCIETY TRUST

FRONTISPIECE

Drawing and calligraphy by Sanpū of one of Basho's haiku,

Tenri Central Library. See haiku 195.

Contents

Foreword

This preface does not intend to provide an introductory guideline to understanding this book's content, namely, the haiku of Basho, nor offer an explanatory remark on the amazing aesthetics manifested in the translation. The introduction signed by both of those to whom we owe this work will certainly adopt these roles excellently. A masterpiece should be protected from being blemished by imperfect commentaries.

The fact that I intend to concentrate on the implications of the finished product, haiku in translation, must not in any way be allowed to draw attention from the fact that this book is the outcome of a true collaboration resulting from a quarter of a century of close, harmonious encounter in the deepest meaning of that term.

Without Professor Kemmyo Taira Sato, with his wide-ranging knowledge and depth of understanding, there would be no haiku in translation and no book. That such a demonstration of the wealth of possibilities inherent in true Anglo-Japanese cooperation, even in such a field, is a possibly somewhat unexpected result of Shogyoji Temple's decision, under Venerable Chimyo Takehara's far-sighted leadership, to set up a subsidiary in London.

Essentially, however, I wish to describe my admiration for the frame of mind with which Professor White approaches the reading of a text in general, as I have perceived it through the exchange of our understanding of Buddhist texts over the last two decades. Highlighting the profundity of the author's astuteness in reading a text would reveal at least a part of the environment from which this wonderful work of art emerges.

Professor John White, a world-renowned authority in the field of art history, has been a most reliable critic on Buddhist scriptures for me. Based on meticulous reading of English translations rendered from several versions written in Sanskrit, Pali, and Classical Chinese, those most likely to be suited to the same origin, he has advanced invaluable suggestions on problems derived from the translator's unconcern for or misapprehension of the worldview of the given text.

Professor White, in reading a text, does not confine his sentiency to the meaning of a translation *per se*, but, going beyond, places it carefully in accord with the fundamental tone of the assumed original text to be discerned through the various modes of diction disseminated in the translation.

His discernment in restructuring the slightest disharmony caused by a misleading rendition owes essentially to his perspicacity in prefiguring the field of meaning that induces any meaning. The prefiguration of the domain of potential meaning prior to language development precedes the translation to be performed as the con-figuration of language.

Professor White's sagacity in understanding Buddhist texts origi-nating in his ingenuity in prefiguring the field of meaning is most likely to accrue from his academic and personal backgrounds; he is an art historian and, simultaneously, a poet, who, in addition, pos-sesses profound experience in the ambience of a living tradition of Japanese Buddhism.

Buddhist texts are replete with various modes of diction such as metaphor, simile, anecdote, paradox, logic, metaphysics, and so on. Understanding such texts requires a highly developed sense of integrity that can place a seemingly disorderly set of discourses in a preconceptual domain, harmoniously. Art history and poetry composition, which strive for the prefiguration of their province through icons and signs, almost producing verbal conceptions, would be appropriate for completing this task.

Professor White's insight in reading Buddhist texts holds squarely true to reading and translating Basho's haiku. I am more inter-ested in haiku than Buddhist texts as they comprise the smallest number of syllables in literary style and are unconstrained by the established doctrines of monastic Buddhism; they provide an arena wherein the author's discernment is demonstrated more precisely and abundantly. The reader will find that this work indeed fulfils this expectation.

Eastern philosophical traditions, in contrast to that of the West, indicate that metaphysics finds its ultimate end in a domain ahead of language. Language loses its original function of semantic denotation at the point where metaphysical thought attains its terminal depth. Metaphysics here denotes the specific sense that nothing is differentiated in this realm of language that is embodied in the moment of negating itself.

This phenomenon of being in unity appears to coincide remarkably with 'a fundamental principle' attested in Western art and architecture that 'form and function are as one'. There is, however, a single distinct difference; unity in Western art is confirmed on the margin of external material, whereas in Eastern metaphysics, occurs in the single domain of a deeper layer of language.

In the latter dimension, therefore, it appears that language can potentially create materiality in the sphere of perception. Certainly, my sheer amazement is because it appears as if Basho's experiences were being vividly re-enacted by my tracing the rhythms and forms of Professor White's English translation, and this is something I have never experienced in the Japanese language thus far.

Masahiro Shimoda
Professor of Buddhist Studies, the University of Tokyo

Introduction

IN THE ORIGINAL JAPANESE, and in the poetry of Matsuo Basho (1644–1694) in particular, the two defining features of a haiku in its purest form are firstly its 5–7–5 sound unit format, the English counterpart of which is a syllable, and secondly its rhythm.

Though often denied, the English counterpart of a haiku in Japanese is therefore a rhythmic 5–7–5 syllabic structure.

Yet strangely enough, in all the major translations of Basho's haiku into English, whether by Japanese or British, or latterly by American authorities, this essential feature is largely ignored and often only now and then occurs, almost as if by chance.

What follows in this selection of three hundred of his haiku is seemingly, therefore, a first attempt to do a strict translation into English haiku of what was actually written, some three hundred and fifty years ago, by the man who is still revered by many as the greatest of all Japanese haiku poets.

It almost goes without saying that in any attempt to translate poetry from one language to another, the translator is faced with two major problems.

The first is that in any language there may be words or phrases or ideas in the one for which there are no direct equivalents in the other.

The second is that in many cases, Japanese and English being one of them, there are widely differing grammatical structures.

In the case of Basho's haiku, his own calligraphy can either take the form of a single, undifferentiated vertical line, as in Plate 2 with the famous poem of the Frog, or often, when associated with a drawing, employ the three line, similarly vertical 5–7–5 format shown in Plates 1, 3, 4, 8 and 15.

Subsequently, following the Meiji Restoration of 1868, a Romanised Script in various forms using a horizontal, three line format was developed as a kind of compromise between East and West which would allow the use of the English alphabet.

In much of Western art and architecture it has been a fundamental principle that form and function are as one, and in its own way the layout of each page in the present volume, with Basho's original at the top, the Romanised transition in the middle, culminating with the new translation at the bottom, reflects the fact.

It must, however, always be remembered that, especially in poetry, a translation can never match the original, but the translator should at least try to respect the discipline, the form and spirit of the poems the author originally wrote. This puts a special emphasis on honouring those elements which are transposable.

Even before it is bodied out in words or turned into a poem, the basic symmetrical format of a haiku, starting at five, rising to seven and then falling back to five, which is not a mere stylistic add-on or convention, but is an essential feature, itself imposes a subtle rhythm that Basho exploits in many different ways and is analogous to the opening rise and fall of a sine wave which, in its full, repetitive oscillations, is so significant a natural phenomenon.

Though often not, in practice, in its purest mathematical form, the sine wave underlies the basic structure of waves in water, sound waves, visible light waves, the movement of a spring that is pulled and released, the vibrations of a plucked guitar string, earthquake and radio waves, the succession of the hours of daylight, and a host of other aspects of the natural world.

In textbooks it is often shown in its steepest, most energetic form, but even in a soft breeze out at sea or on a lake, or in the gentle undulations from a long-gone, great storm a thousand miles beyond the horizon, it is there.

Brought up with a delight in nature that may well be related to the Shinto cultural background of Japan, and later intensified by that deep-seated feeling for the unity of all that is and is not, which lies at the very heart of Buddhism, it is therefore no surprise that Basho should instinctively have found in haiku the ideal way to express his lifelong passion.

This leads back again to an emphasis on the second defining feature of a haiku, namely its rhythm.

Although Basho himself seldom departed from the norm, and even then tended to add or subtract no more than a single syllable or so, he was certainly no pedant, and on one occasion wrote to a disciple saying that "Even if you have three or four extra sound units – or as many as five or seven – you need not worry as long as the verse sounds right. If even one sound unit stagnates in your mouth, give it a careful scrutiny."

What he was writing about was the overriding importance in a haiku of its rhythmic structure.

Unfortunately the vast majority of his translators have taken Basho's lack of pedantry too much to heart.

In virtually all of the major English publications of his poetry, it is only now and then that the normative 5-7-5 pattern is strictly adhered to, and consistently to drop, at one extreme, from seventeen syllables to ten or twelve or so, or even to go down as low as six or seven, with an entire line being taken up by a single, one or two syllable word, is to lose all hope of finding a counterpart for Basho's fundamental rhythms.

At the other extreme, to turn to a regular four line format, often with twenty-two to twenty-five syllables or more, is once more to lose contact with the very essence and characteristic brevity of Basho's own poetry.

In all the translations that follow in this particular selection of Basho's haiku, the 5-7-5 format is strictly adhered to, and whenever Basho does see fit to add or subtract a sound unit or two in a given line, the syllabic structure of the resulting English haiku meticulously follows the same pattern.

In this connection, full account has always to be taken of the fact that, Japanese poetry being organised in terms of the mora, denoting the common short foot, instead of that of the syllable, the addition of a superscribed macron to a vowel in Japanese, as for example in *chō*, has the effect of making it count as two moras or sound units instead of one, and therefore, in translation, of adding another syllable to the line concerned.

Another feature of Japanese which may be a source of confusions is that whenever the consonant 'n' is not followed by a vowel, it counts by itself as one mora, and therefore in English, once more adds a further syllable to the line involved. In addition, whenever a consonant is doubled, it counts as two moras in Japanese or two syllables in English, while any sequence of plain vowels becomes a similar number of syllables in translation.

Moreover, since, as can be seen in the single, vertical lines of the original Japanese script of some of Basho's haiku, apart from there being no capitals, there are no gaps or capital letters, or other purely visual indications of the essential structure of the poems, and there is also no punctuation as such, the latter has been kept to what has seemed to be a sensible, rather than absolute minimum in the translations which follow.

Over and above the more technical matters, there is the flow of ideas as a poetic thought develops.

In Basho's haiku in particular, the line-by-line sequence plays an extremely complex role, not only in varying, but also in extending the range of meanings in what might otherwise seem to be a highly restricted poetic form.

Every effort has therefore been made to maintain, as far as possible, not only the syllabic structure and rhythm, but also the linear sequence of ideas from one line to the next in the three lines of each haiku.

As it turns out there are, in what follows, only a small handful of cases in which it has seemed necessary to alter the line-by-line sequence of the originals because of the very different structure of the two languages.

The commonplace that, in historical terms, each haiku must have a seasonal connection seems simple enough and is true of the vast majority of the output of Basho himself and of his contemporaries and his successors, such as Yosa Buson and Kobayashi Issa in the succeeding centuries.

In fact, however, especially when it comes to translation, it hides a multiplicity of problems.

For a start, there is the inescapable complication that in the lunar calendar of Basho's day, which controlled not only the seasons, but the dates of all the festivals and other annual activities, the year began in February, so that on occasion a given month can be associated with a different season from that accepted in the solar system now used in the western world.

To give just one example, the eighth month, which is August and in seasonal terms belongs to summer, runs from early September to early October in the lunar calendar and is therefore seen as part of autumn.

In addition, it must be remembered that sharp dividing lines between the seasons, as in poetry and elsewhere, are simply conventions, whereas in nature itself they slide imperceptibly into one another.

The seasonal placement of a haiku is, on the contrary, governed by a strictly adhered to system of marker words, the moon, for instance, always being autumnal unless some qualification is added or the context indicates otherwise, while fleas are confined to summer, which is hardly the case in nature.

Even then there can be surprises, since on one occasion, haiku 164 in this collection, Basho suddenly turns to another, less used system in which the year is divided into twenty-four more or less equal sections.

In the light of all this we have, in what follows, sometimes added a note where the divergence between the lunar and solar calendars seemed to call for it, and the seasons, marked by illustrations almost all of them coming from Basho himself, are roughly set out in a four-year cycle, which gives the transitions, continuities and contrasts between the winter at the end of one year and the spring at the beginning of the next their due value, which is not of course the case when they are separated from each other at the far ends of the passage of a single year.

The haiku have as far as possible been allotted to the various seasons in accordance with the dictates of the Japanese marker words, though in a few cases a 'spring' haiku has been set one or two places into summer or vice versa, and a small handful, because of their poetic content and connections, have been deliberately moved, for better or worse, from their conventional seasonal positions.

Apart from problems such as these, a particular aspect of Basho's haiku, which often passes unremarked, is their relationship to synaesthesia, which in western terms, is a neurological phenomenon in which the stimulation of one sensory or cognitive pathway is invariably accompanied by involuntary experiences in another.

It comes in many forms; each sound may actually be seen, not merely thought of, as a colour, every colour have a smell, each fragrance have a sound, the call of a distant deer be seen as being only one inch high.

There is no evidence that Basho and the other haiku poets who shared similar sensitivities to the natural world, had this unusual neurological deviation from the norm. In certain cases there may indeed be a straightforward historical derivation, white being the colour of autumn in the ancient Taoist system of correspondences familiar in Japan.

On the other hand, it is quite possible that, in general, their apparent synaesthesia stems from a deeply felt awareness of the central Buddhist concept of the unity of all that is.

That unity of course has each and every one of the five senses in its ambit.

Curiously enough the trajectory of Basho's own short life echoes the trajectory of the spiritual development of the nation as a whole in the course of the preceding couple of millennia.

The source of Basho's own passionate relationship with the world of nature lies, of course, far deeper than the simple fact that Japan was and still is a land of forests, mountains and volcanoes, of fast flowing streams and rivers while, in Basho's day, the twenty per cent or so of the land mass that was flat enough was largely given over to agriculture.

Another way of looking at late seventeenth-century Japan is to see it as a land of Shinto shrines and Buddhist temples, yet in spite of this the part which his religious affiliations and intense spiritual life played in his poetry has often, for various reasons and not only in the West, been severely downplayed or actually denied.

Born the son of a seemingly low level samurai in the small town of Ueno which, with its samurai quarter, its Shinto shrine and its Buddhist temples, which Basho would also have known well, was dominated by the feudal castle with its unusually precipitous walls that was completed in the second half of the sixteenth century.

Basho remained in Ueno until 1266, when he was twenty-two, and the lasting and profound effect that these surroundings had on him is shown, some thirteen years later, when he dedicated his book, *The Shell Game* (*Kai ōi*), which he wrote and bound himself, to the Shinto shrine in his home town.

The origins of Shinto, which is native to Japan, lie in the country's prehistoric past and in the animist beliefs in which each tree, each rock, each mountain is possessed of a living, individual spirit in the form of a resident god or kami.

It clearly played a major role in the very special Japanese relationship to the natural world, which was evident in Basho's day and which derived fresh impetus, a firm philosophical basis, and its own particular flavour, following the arrival of Buddhism in the course of the sixth century AD, and it is very probably the wellspring for his own particular love of nature.

It is not simply that, as time went by, in every district Buddhist temples proliferated alongside Shinto shrines and came to be the dominant feature of Japan's religious landscape.

By its very nature Shinto was essentially local. In sharp contrast to Buddhism it possessed no literature, no centuries of written history or elaborate religious theory, and no overarching organisation linking one shrine with the next.

As a result not only did the two faiths for the most part live quite happily side by side at a local level, but a surprisingly high proportion of the Shinto shrines were actually, in practice, run by local Buddhist priests.

As far as Basho's personal spiritual journey was concerned, he seems to have spent some time in Kyoto after leaving Ueno, before moving on to Edo, but the crucial turning point appears to have come in 1680 when his students built a cottage for him in Fukagawa on the outskirts of the town.

It was then that he began a period of serious training under the Zen master, Butchō, and the powers of concentration involved in the practice of deep meditation show themselves time and time again in his haiku in the intensity and perseverance which he applied to the observation of even the smallest and most detailed aspect of the plant and insect life by which he was surrounded or to the long, repeated periods of moon watching.

At one time it seems that he even thought of entering the monastic life, but decided in the end to devote himself exclusively to poetry.

This by no means meant that Buddhism was left behind, and his Zen training helped to ensure that his approach was wholly non-sectarian, the references in several of his haiku to the *nenbutsu* revealing his acquaintance with and his respect for Shin Buddhism, which was from the beginning far removed in the nature of its faith and practices from the established forms of monastic Buddhism.

His endless travels in search of poetic inspiration led him to visit and to pray in a multitude of different shrines and temples, and although he never in fact became a monk, he did on occasion shave his head and wear a monk's robes on his journeys simply to indicate that he was not worth robbing and to ease his way through the innumerable checkpoints on the road.

What did remain with him as a vivid feature of his entire life were certain Buddhist fundamentals.

His starting point in Shinto was clearly given new dimensions and new depth in the light of the Buddhist concept of the unity of all that is and is not, in which all hierarchies and distinctions, all the separations between one aspect of the natural world and another, simply fade away; the call of a distant deer and the deer itself have ceased to be separate.

This undoubtedly intensified the thoroughgoing anthropomorphism which was evident from the start in Basho's poetry and which can at first seem rather strange in Western eyes, and is certainly foreign to modern scientific ways of thinking.

Basho's poetry is full of firefly, cherry blossom and moon-viewing, and of the acceptance that such natural entities as spiders, butterflies, cicadas, trees and fleas and flowers, and ourselves, are equals that can constantly converse.

In his haiku there is nothing strange in his calling out to butterflies for their companionship or in asking a spider what sort of song it is proposing to sing in the autumn breeze; if he can weep then there can be tears in fishes' eyes as well at spring's departure.

In cosmic matters, at the other end of the scale, the moon was never far from Basho and the clear sound of the fulling block, as it beat the cloth that was being softened, carried up to the Great Bear.

With this all-inclusiveness, and his concern for the shortness of the lives of insects and of birds alike, there came an intensified awareness of the impermanence of all created things, another fundamental Buddhist concept.

This gives a particular poignancy to such haiku as the two that speak of the cicadas singing on in the sunshine, unaware of the imminence of death at the end of so short a life, or of the bush warbler trilling of its old age amongst the burgeoning shoots of new life in the spring.

For Basho, morning glory flowers, Buddhist priests and fish alike were covered by the net of the *dharma,* as indeed was every living thing.

Some awareness of the complex interrelationships in Basho's personality, and of his deep-seated religious beliefs, can only lead to a more intense feeling for his poetry and a better understanding of his whole approach to nature and to life itself.

But Basho was a poet, not a preacher, and he took no part in philosophical or doctrinal arguments.

He did not need to, since, with few exceptions, everything he wrote was imbued with his intensely felt Buddhist faith.

Indeed, there are only a very few of his haiku in which there are specific references to Buddhist belief through their mention of such things as the *nenbutsu* or the *dharma*.

His way is much more subtle and profound, not merely more poetic, and is well illustrated by the haiku at the midpoint of this book, which, in the brief compass of no more than seventeen syllables, is concerned with emptiness, that fundamental Buddhist belief that nothing, we ourselves included, has a permanent, inherent self.

kozue yori
adani ochi keri
semi no kara

out of a treetop
it was emptiness that fell;
a cicada shell

The Haiku

PLATE 1
Drawing by Kyoriku, calligraphy by Basho,
Tenri Central Library. See haiku 1.

1.

ほろ〳〵と山吹ちるか瀧の音

horo horo to
yamabuki chiru ka
taki no oto

yellow rose petals
gently, gently flutter down;
waterfall thunder

2.

kirishigure
fuji o mi nu hi zo
omoshiroki

mist and gentle rain,
fuji can't be seen today;
how fascinating!

3.

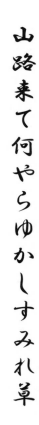

yamaji kite
naniyara yukashi
sumire-gusa

on a mountain path,
to catch sight of violets
is somehow touching

4.

永き日を囀りたらぬ雲雀かな

nagaki hi o
saezuri tara nu
hibari kana

throughout a long day
with never a pause at all,
a skylark in song

5.

菜畠に花見顔なる雀哉

na-batake ni
hanami-gao naru
suzume kana

in a field of rape
with flower viewing faces,
a flock of sparrows

6.

岩躑躅染る泪やほとゝぎ朱

iwatsutsuji
somuru namida ya
hototogisu

rock azaleas
so it seems, have been dyed red
by the cuckoos' tears

7.

haru nare ya
na mo naki yama no
asagasumi

the spring has arrived;
on the hill that has no name
there is morning mist

8.

むめがゝにのつと日の出る山路かな

mume ga ka ni
notto hi no deru
yamaji kana

amid plum tree scent
the sun suddenly came up
on the mountain path

samidare ni
kakure nu mono ya
seta no hashi

in the rains of may
the only thing still in sight
the bridge at seta

*1

10.

風吹けば尾ぼそうなるや犬櫻

kaze fuke ba
obosō naru ya
inuzakura

as white blossoms blow
away in the wind, the trees
appear to dwindle

11.

春かぜやきせるくはへて船頭殿

harukaze ya
kiseru kuwaete
sendo-dono

a pipe in his mouth,
mister boatman is smoking;
a breeze in springtime

12.

青柳の泥にしだるゝ塩干かな

aoyagi no
doro ni shidaruru
shiohi kana

the green willow trees
are dripping into the mud
now the tide is out

13.

ほとゝぎす消行方や島一ツ

hototogisu
kieyuku kata ya
shima hitotsu

where a small cuckoo
disappeared in the distance,
a single island

*2

14.

世にゝほへ梅花一枝のみそさゞい

yo ni nioe
baika isshi no
misosazai

a sweet-scented world;
on a branch of plum blossom
a wren is perching

15.

古池や蛙飛こむ水のをと

furuike ya
kawazu tobikomu
mizu no oto

by an ancient pond
a frog leaping into it;
the sound of water

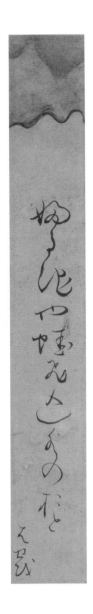

PLATE 2

Calligraphy by Basho,

Kakimori Bunko Foundation. See haiku 15.

16.

hatsu makuwa
yotsu ni ya wara n
wa ni kira n

the year's first melon;
how should i cut it; in four
or in round slices

17.

五月雨に鶴の足みじかくなれり

samidare ni
tsuru no ashi
mijikaku nare ri

heavy summer rain
has caused the cranes' legs
to be very much shorter

18.

shiogoshi ya
tsuru hagi nurete
umi suzushi

crossing at low tide
the legs of the cranes are wet
with the sea's coolness

*3

19.

さざれ蟹足はひのぼる清水哉

sazaregani
ashi hainoboru
shimizu kana

a very small crab
has found its way up my leg
in clear stream water

20.

原中や物にもつかず鳴雲雀

hara-naka ya
mono ni mo tsuka zu
naku hibari

out over the plain
free of any attachment,
the skylarks, singing

21.

あやめ草足にむすばん草鞋の緒

ayame-gusa
ashi ni musuba n
waraji no o

irises, it seems,
are blossoming on my feet;
sandals laced with blue

22.

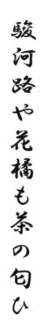

surugaji ya
hana tachibana mo
cha no nioi

on the suruga
road, orange blossom scent mixed
with that of the tea

*4

23.

shizukasa ya
iwa ni shimiiru
semi no koe

amid the stillness
the rocks are penetrated
by cicada songs

24.

木啄も庵はやぶらず夏木立

kitsutsuki mo
io wa yabura zu
natsu-kodachi

even woodpeckers
do not harm this little hut
among summer trees

*5

25.

梢よりあだに落けり蝉のから

kozue yori
adani ochi keri
semi no kara

out of a treetop
it was emptiness that fell;
a cicada shell

26.

僧朝顔幾死かえる法の松

sō asagao
iku shini kaeru
nori no matsu

monks and morning glories,
dying again and again;
the dharma pine tree

*6

頓て死ぬけしきは見えず蝉の聲

yagate shinu
keshiki wa mie zu
semi no koe

they will die so soon,
yet there is no thought of it
in cicadas' songs

28.

夏草や兵共がゆめの跡

natsukusa ya
tsuwamono domo ga
yume no ato

the summer grasses;
of warriors' ambitions
all that now remains

29.

湖やあつさをおしむ雲のみね

mizuumi ya
atsusa o oshimu
kumo no mine

high over the lake
missing the heat of summer,
soaring peaks of cloud

30.

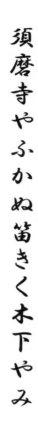

sumadera ya
fuka nu fue kiku
koshitayami

in sumadera
i heard the unblown flute sing
in the trees' deep shade

*7

53

31.

有難や雪をかほらす南谷

arigata ya
yuki o kaorasu
minamidani

how grateful i am
to breathe this snow scented air;
minamidani

*8

32.

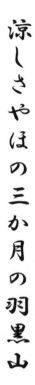

suzushisa ya
hono mikazuki no
haguroyama

what coolness; a faint
crescent moon shining down now
on haguro-san

*9

33.

ほとゝぎす大竹籔をもる月夜

hototogisu
ō takeyabu o
moru tsukiyo

a cuckoo calling;
down through the vast bamboo grove
filters the moonlight

34.

涼しさを我宿にしてねまる也

suzushisa o
waga yado ni shite
nemaru nari

making the coolness
become my own dwelling place,
i stay for a rest

35.

粽結ふかた手にはさむ額髪

chimaki yuu
katate ni hasamu
hitaigami

wrapping rice dumplings,
she uses one hand to push
her forelock aside

36.

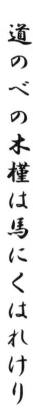

michinobe no
mukuge wa uma ni
kuwa re keri

there by the roadside
a rose of sharon flower
eaten by my horse

野を横に馬牽むけよほとゝぎす

no o yoko ni
uma hikimuke yo
hototogisu

crossing the moorland
on horseback we turn its head
to the cuckoo's call

38.

秣負ふ人を枝折の夏野哉

magusa ou
hito o shiori no
natsuno kana

people with fodder
on their backs are as signposts
on the summer moor

39.

闇の夜や巣をまどはしてなく衝

yami no yo ya
su o madowashite
naku chidori

in the night's darkness
a plover sings, disguising
its nest's position

40.

*ikameshiki
oto ya arare no
hinoki-gasa*

**how harsh is the sound
that is made by the hailstones
on my cypress hat**

*10

PLATE 3
Drawing and calligraphy by Basho,
Three Wheels Temple. See haiku 40.

41.

いなづまや闇の方行五位の聲

inazuma ya
yami no kata yuku
goi no koe

a flash of lightning!
flying into the darkness
a night heron calls

42.

此
道
や
行
人
な
し
に
秋
の
暮

kono michi ya
yuku hito nashi ni
aki no kure

along this pathway
there is no one that travels
in autumn twilight

43.

野ざらしを心に風のしむ身哉

nozarashi o
kokoro ni kaze no
shimu mi kana

resigned to dying
from exposure, how the wind
cuts its way through me!

44.

刈あとや早稲かた〳〵の鴫の聲

kari ato ya
wase katakata no
shigi no koe

in harvested fields
of early rice, here and there
the sound of a snipe

*11

45.

inoshishi no
toko ni mo iru ya
kirigirisu

a wild boar it seems
is prepared to share its bed
with a cricket too

46.

曙や霧にうずまく鐘の聲

akebono ya
kiri ni uzumaku
kane no koe

in morning half-light
swirling its way through the mist
the sound of a bell

47.

kiku no hana
saku ya ishiya no
ishi no ai

chrysanthemums bloom
in a mason's yard between
all the blocks of stone

48.

芭蕉葉を柱にかけん庵の月

bashō-ba o
hashira ni kake n
io no tsuki.

let's hang banana
leaves on the hermitage post
to look at the moon

49.

名月の花かと見へて綿畠

meigetsu no
hana ka to miete
wata batake

under the full moon
what appeared to be flowers
were fields of cotton

50.

よき家や雀よろこぶ背戸の粟

yoki ie ya
suzume yorokobu
sedo no awa

a very nice house;
sparrows enjoy the millet
in the field beyond

51.

稲雀茶の木畠や逃どころ

ina-suzume
cha no ki batake ya
nigedokoro

for rice-field sparrows
the tea plantations offer
a place of safety

52.

草の戸をしれや穂蓼に唐がらし

kusa no to o
shire ya hotade ni
tōgarashi

at the grassy gate
are flowers of red pepper
and water pepper

53.

牛部やに蚊の聲よはし秋の風

ushibeya ni
ka no koe yowashi
aki no kaze

in the cattle shed,
mosquitoes' buzzing grows faint;
the winds of autumn

54.

浪の間や子貝にまじる萩の塵

nami no ma ya
kogai ni majiru
hagi no chiri

in between the waves
in among the small seashells,
bush clover petals

55.

海士の屋は小海老にまじるいとゞ哉

ama no ya wa
koebi ni majiru
itodo kana

a fisherman's hut;
mixed in amongst the small shrimps
there are crickets too

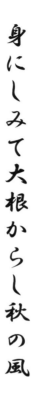

mi ni shimite
daikon karashi
aki no kaze

the bitter radish
bites me and in it i feel
the wind of autumn

57.

芭蕉野分して盥に雨を聞夜かな

bashō nowaki shite
tarai ni ame o
kiku yo kana

banana tree in autumn storm,
rain dripping into the tubs;
listening all night

58.

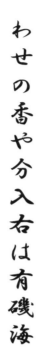

wase no ka ya
wakeiru migi wa
ariso umi

an early rice smell
going in, and on the right
a beach with rough surf

59.

賤のこやいね摺掛けて月をみる

shizu no ko ya
ine surikakete
tsuki o miru

a peasant's young child
hulling rice, has stopped working
to look at the moon

60.

荒海や佐渡によこたふ天河

araumi ya
sado ni yokotō
ama no gawa

tempestuous sea;
arching over to sado
flows the milky way

*13

61.

比良みかみ雪指わたせ鷺の橋

hira mikami
yuki sashiwatase
sagi no hashi

hira, mikami;
between snow covered mountains
a bridge of egrets

*14

62.

かれ朶に烏のとまりけり秋の暮

kare-eda ni
karasu no tomari keri
aki no kure

on a tree's dead branch
a crow has settled itself to roost;
twilight in autumn

PLATE 4
Drawing by Kyoriku, calligraphy by Basho,
Idemitsu Museum. See haiku 62.

87

63.

時雨をやもどかしがりて松の雪

shigure o ya
modokashi-garite
matsu no yuki

a winter shower
is an irritating thing
for snow covered pines

64.

冬がれや世は一色に風のをと

fuyugare ya
yo wa hito iro ni
kaze no oto

winter withering,
everything one colour;
the roar of the wind

65.

瓶破るゝよるの氷の寝覚哉

kame waruru
yoru no kōri no
nezame kana

a water jar burst
when icing up in the night;
i suddenly woke

66.

炉開や左官老行鬢の霜

robiraki ya
sakan oiyuku
bin no shimo

fireplace opening;
the plasterer's getting old,
frost on his side locks

67.

shiore fusu ya
yo wa sakasama no
yuki no take

being bowed down so low,
a world that is upside down;
snow on the bamboos

68.

kogarashi ya
take ni kakurete
shizumari nu

the cold winter winds
hid themselves in the bamboos
and then became still

69.

君火たけよき物みせむ雪丸

kimi hi take
yoki mono mise n
yukimaruge

if you light a fire
i will show you something good,
a large ball of snow

70.

明ぼのやしら魚しろきこと一寸

akebono ya
shirauo shiroki
koto issun

in the dawn's half-light
the icefish shows its whiteness,
only an inch long

71.

ariake mo
misoka ni chikashi
mochi no oto

a pale morning moon
marks the year's end to the sound
of pounding steamed rice

PLATE 5
Drawing by Kyoriku, calligraphy by Basho,
Yamadera Basho Memorial Museum. See haiku 72.

72.

春もやゝけしきとゝのふ月と梅

haru mo yaya
keshiki totonou
tsuki to ume

now the springtime scene
is almost prepared once more;
plum blossoms, moonlight

73.

庭はきて雪をわするゝはゝきかな

niwa hakite
yuki o wasururu
hahaki kana

sweeping the garden,
the broom has quite forgotten
the snow that was there

74.

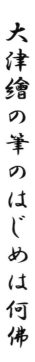

ōtsu-e no
fude no hajime wa
nani botoke

painters in otsu
now start the first brush drawings;
what sort of buddha

75.

furudera no
momo ni kome fumu
otoko kana

at an old temple
the peach trees are blossoming,
a man pounding rice

*16

76.

うたがふな潮の花も浦の春

utagau na
ushio no hana mo
ura no haru

have no doubts at all;
with the flowers of the tide
the bay has its spring

77.

樫
の
木
の
花
に
か
ま
は
ぬ
姿
か
な

kashi no ki no
hana ni kamawa nu
sugata kana

the evergreen oak
does not care about flowers,
that is its nature

78.

咲き乱す桃の中より初櫻

saki midasu
momo no naka yori
hatsu-zakura

peaches in full bloom
and among them cherry trees
with their first blossoms

79.

よくみれば薺花さく垣ねかな

yoku mireba
nazuna hana saku
kakine kana

if you look with care,
a shepherd's purse is in bloom
under the hedgerow

80.

uguisu ya
take-no-ko yabu ni
oi o naku

a bush warbler there
in the bamboo grove's new shoots
sings of its old age

81.

花の雲鐘は上野か浅草歟

hana no kumo
kane wa ueno ka
asakusa ka

cherry blossom clouds;
is that bell in ueno
or asakusa

*17

82.

世にさかる花にも念佛申しけり

yo ni sakaru
hana ni mo nebutsu
mōshi keri

cherries in blossom;
also to them *nenbutsu*
has been recited

*18

83.

しばらくは花の上なる月夜かな

shibaraku wa
hana no ue naru
tsukiyo kana

for a little while
the night's moon is just over
the cherry blossom

84.

木のもとに汁も膾も櫻かな

ki no moto ni
shiru mo namasu mo
sakura kana

underneath the tree
in the soup and fish salad,
petals of cherry

85.

花にねぬ此もたぐいか鼠の巣

hana ni ne nu
kore mo tagui ka
nezumi no su

looking at blossoms
my now being kept awake
is a nest of mice

yuku haru ya
tori naki uo no
me wa namida

spring is departing
and all the birds are weeping;
tears in fishes' eyes

PLATE 6

Drawing by Sekishi, calligraphy by Basho,

Tenri Central Library. See haiku 88.

87.

しばらくは瀧に籠もるや夏の始

shiburaku wa
taki ni komoru ya
ge no hajime

shut for a short while
behind the falls, i will start
the summer retreat

*19

88.

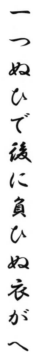

hitotsu nuide
ushiro ni oi nu
koromogae

taking one garment off
and putting it on my back,
that's the change of clothes

89.

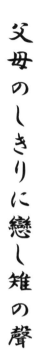

chichi haha no
shikiri ni koishi
kiji no koe

father and mother,
how often i long for them
as a pheasant calls

90.

霧雨の空を芙蓉の天気哉

kirisame no
sora o fuyō no
tenki kana

with a misty rain
in the sky, the rose mallows
enjoy the weather

91.

hototogisu
naku ya go shaku no
ayamegusa

the lesser cuckoo
sings in the sky above five
feet tall irises

92.

takenoko ya
osanaki toki no
e no susabi

a bamboo shoot, when
i was young my favourite
subject for a sketch

93.

雀子と聲鳴かはす鼠の巣

suzume-go to
koe nakikawasu
nezumi no su

the baby sparrows
are exchanging their greetings
with a nest of mice

94.

我宿は蚊のちいさきを馳走かな

waga yado wa
ka no chiisaki o
chisō kana

in my dwelling place
small mosquitoes are the best
i can offer you

95.

花は賤のめにもみえけり鬼薊

hana wa shizu no
me ni mo miekeri
oniazami

for all the poor people
the flowers that catch their eye
are the plumed thistles

96.

kogakurete
chatsumi mo kiku ya
hototogisu

hidden by bushes
do the tea-pickers listen
to lesser cuckoos

97.

鐘消て花の香は撞夕哉

kane kiete
hana no ka wa tsuku
yūbe kana

the bell's sound dies down,
the flowers' scent rising up
it is evening

98.

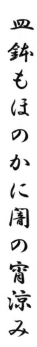

sara bachi mo
honokani yami no
yoisuzumi

the plates and the bowls
are still faintly to be seen
in evening's cool

99.

ふるすただあはれなるべき隣かな

furusu tada
aware naru beki
tonari kana

only an old nest,
how lonely it could become,
that neighbouring house

100.

ki o kirite
motokuchi miru ya
kyō no tsuki

the cleanly sawn end
of a tree that is just felled;
the disk of tonight's moon

101.

kumo ori ori
hito o yasumeru
tsukimi kana

once in a while a cloud
arrives and gives some respite
to the moon viewers

102.

山も庭もうごき入るや夏坐敷

yama mo niwa mo
ugoki iruru ya
natsu zashiki

the garden and mountains
move into the sitting room
during the summer

103.

ひやひやと壁をふまへて昼寝哉

hiya hiya to
kabe o fumaete
hirune kana

i feel the coolness
with my feet against the wall
for a midday nap

104.

蜻蛉やとりつきかねし草の上

tonbō ya
toritsuki kane shi
kusa no ue

a dragonfly tried
but in vain, to settle down
on a blade of grass

すゞしさを繪にうつしけり嵯峨の竹

suzushisa o
e ni utsushi keri
saga no take

the coolness itself
has become a brush drawing;
bamboos of saga!

*20

106.

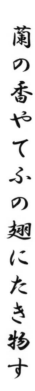

ran no ka ya
chō no tsubasa ni
takimono su

**a scented orchid
washes a butterfly's wings
with its own perfume**

107.

夕にも朝にもつかず瓜の花

yūbe ni mo
asa ni mo tsuka zu
uri no hana

it is not confined
to morning or evening,
the melon flower

108.

暑き日を海にいれたり最上川

atsuki hi o
umi ni ire tari
mogami-gawa

it sweeps the burning
sun down into the ocean;
mogami river

*21

135

109.

蛍見や船頭酔ておぼつかな

hotaru mi ya
sendō yōte
obotsukana

out firefly viewing
along with an unsteady
boatman that is drunk

110.

hototogisu
naku naku tobu zo
isogawashi

the lesser cuckoo,
calling, calling, and flying;
what a busy life!

111.

風流の初やおくの田植うた

fūryū no
hajime ya oku no
taueuta

it seems elegance
had beginnings in oku
in rice planting songs

*22

112.

降ずとも竹植る日や蓑と笠

furazu tomo
take uuru hi ya
mino to kasa

even with no rain
on bamboo-planting day; straw
coat and bamboo hat

113.

さざ波や風の薫の相拍子

sazanami ya
kaze no kaori no
ai byōshi

among rippling waves
the fragrance of blowing wind
is in their rhythm

114.

五月雨に鳰の浮巣を見に行む

samidare ni
nio no uki su o
mi ni yuka n

in this summer rain
the floating nest of a grebe
i shall go to see

115.

此ほたる田ごとの月にくらべみん

kono hotaru
tagoto no tsuki ni
kurabe mi n

i like to compare
these fireflies to all the moons
in the rice paddies

116.

畫見れば首筋赤きほたる哉

hiru mire ba
kubisuji akaki
hotaru kana

by the light of day
the nape of a firefly's neck
is seen to be red

117.

桑や花なき蝶の世すて酒

kuwa no mi ya
hana naki chō no
yosute-zake

the mulberry fruit
with no blooms for butterflies
is a hermit's wine

PLATE 7
Drawing by Buson,
Kakimori Bunko Foundation.

145

118.

塚も動け我泣聲は秋の風

tsuka mo ugoke
waga naku koe wa
aki no kaze

move, oh burial mound!
the sound of my wailing voice
is the autumn wind

*23

146

119.

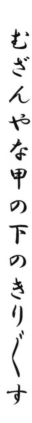

muzan ya na
kabuto no shita no
kirigirisu

how woeful it is;
under a brave man's helmet
a cricket singing

120.

苔埋む蔦のうつゝの念佛哉

koke uzumu
tsuta no utsutsu no
nebutsu kana

out of the mosses
buried in ivy a true
***nenbutsu* is heard**

121.

手にとらば消えんなみだぞあつき秋の霜

te ni toraba kien
namida zo atsuki
aki no shimo

were i to take it in my hand
it would melt in my hot tears
like frost in autumn

*25

122.

稲妻にさとらぬ人の貴さよ

inazuma ni
satora nu hito no
tōtosa yo

seeing the lightning
but remaining unconcerned,
how noble that is

123.

蜘何と音をなにと鳴秋の風

kumo nan to
ne o nani to naku
aki no kaze

spider, with what voice
and in what tones do you sing
in this autumn breeze

124.

asa na asa na
tenarai susumu
kirigirisu

morning in, morning out,
trying to do it better,
the crickets practise

125.

声すみて北斗にひゞく砧哉

koe sumite
hokuto ni hibiku
kinuta kana

clear, echoing sound
rises up to the great bear
from the fulling block

*26

126.

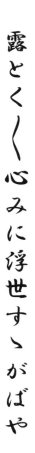

tsuyu toku toku
kokoromi ni ukiyo
susuga baya

the drip, drip of the dew
trying to see this fleeting world
is given a rinse

127.

桟やいのちをからむつたかづら

kakehashi ya
inochi o karamu
tsuta kazura

on the hanging bridge,
intertwining their living
are shoots of ivy

128.

鬼灯は實も葉もからも紅葉哉

hōzuki wa
mi mo ha mo kara mo
momiji kana

the lantern plant's leaves
its fruit and their shells all have
autumnal colours

129.

留主のまにあれたる神の落葉哉

rusu no ma ni
are taru kami no
ochiba kana

all is deserted
the kami's away, dead leaves
are everywhere

130.

百歳の気色を庭の落葉哉

momotose no
keshiki o niwa no
ochiba kana

a century old
this temple garden now looks
with its fallen leaves

131.

一家に遊女もねたり萩と月

hitotsu ya ni
yūjo mo ne tari
hagi to tsuki

under the same roof
there were courtesans sleeping;
a bush clover moon

132.

烏賊賣の聲まぎらはし杜宇

ika uri no
koe magirawashi
hototogisu

cuttlefish sellers'
cries are mingling with the call
of the lesser cuckoo

133.

鶴鳴や其聲に芭蕉やれぬべし

tsuru naku ya
sono koe ni bashō
yare nu beshi

the screech of a crane
could cause the banana tree leaves
to be torn apart

134.

猪もともに吹るゝ野分かな

inoshishi mo
tomo ni fukaruru
nowaki kana

even the wild boars
are blown along at full pelt
by the autumn gales

135.

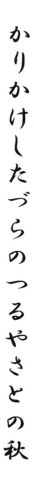

kari kake shi
tazura no tsuru ya
sato no aki

with harvest starting,
the cranes are in the rice fields;
a village in autumn

136.

名月や池をめぐりて夜もすがら

meigetsu ya
ike o megurite
yo mo sugara

an autumn full moon;
so i paced around the pond
the whole of the night

137.

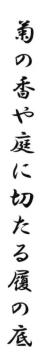

kiku no ka ya
niwa ni kire taru
kutsu no soko

**chrysanthemum scent;
in the garden the worn out
sole of a sandal**

里ふりて柿の木もたぬ家もなし

sato furite
kaki no ki mota nu
ie mo nashi

the hamlet is old,
there is not one house that lacks
a persimmon tree

139.

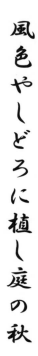

kazairo ya
shidoro ni ue shi
niwa no aki

**the colour of wind
has been planted at random;
an autumn garden**

140.

夜ル竊ニ虫は月下の栗を穿ツ

yoru hisoka ni
mushi wa gekka no
kuri o ugatsu

in night-time secrecy
under the moon, a worm
bores into a chestnut

141.

日にかゝる雲やしばしのわたりどり

hi ni kakaru
kumo ya shibashi no
watari dori

for a time the sun
is hidden behind the clouds
of migrating birds

142.

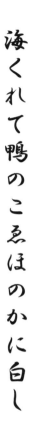

umi kurete
kamo no koe
honoka ni shiroshi

the sea has darkened,
calls of the wild ducks
have now become faintly white

*27

143.

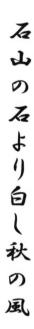

ishiyama no
ishi yori shiroshi
aki no kaze

more white than the stone
seen at stone mountain temple,
the winds of autumn

*28

144.

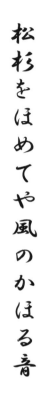

matsu sugi o
home teya kaze no
kaoru oto

pine trees and cedars
are praised by the blowing wind
and its fragrant sound

145.

鶏の声にしぐるゝ牛屋かな

niwatori no
koe ni shigururu
ushiya kana

a cock is crowing
as late autumn rain falls down
on the cowshed roof

146.

しら露もこぼさぬ萩のうねり哉

shiratsuyu mo
kobosa nu hagi no
uneri kana

the white drops of dew
are not spilled by bush clovers
for all their swaying

PLATE 8
Drawing by Sanpū, calligraphy by Basho,
Tenri Central Library. See haiku 147.

175

147.

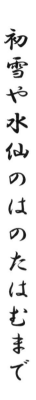

hatsuyuki ya
suisen no ha no
tawamu made

the first snow has come
making the daffodils' leaves
bend under its weight

148.

hatsushigure
saru mo komino o
hoshi ge nari

the first winter rains;
small straw cloaks are what monkeys
seem to be wanting

149.

笠もなき我を時雨るゝか何と〳〵

kasa mo naki
ware o shigururu ka
nanto nanto

not even a hat
when rained on in winter time!
oh dear me, oh dear me!

150.

冬籠りまたよりそはん此はしら

fuyugomori
mata yorisowa n
kono hashira

winter seclusion,
and i shall recline once more
against the same post

月雪とのさばりけらしとしの昏

tsuki yuki to
nosabari kerashi
toshi no kure

i talk 'moon and snow'
with such heedless arrogance
right to the year's end

152.

鞍壺に小坊主のせて大根ひき

kuratsubo ni
kobōzu nosete
daikohiki

**with a small boy left
on the packsaddle, they pull
the white radishes**

153.

木枯に岩吹とがる杉間かな

kogarashi ni
iwa fukitogaru
sugima kana

a withering wind
as it blows, sharpens the rocks
between the cedars

154.

櫓の声波ヲうつて腸氷ル夜やなみだ

ro no koe nami o utte
harawata kōru
yo ya namida

the sound made by the oars slapping the waves;
such a bowel-freezing night,
and tears in my eyes

155.

水寒く寝入かねたるかもめかな

mizu samuku
neiri kane taru
kamome kana

in water so cold
to drop off to sleep is hard
even for seagulls

156.

油こほりともし火細き寝覚哉

abura kōri
tomoshibi hosoki
nezame kana

with the oil frozen
the lamplight becoming dim,
i woke from my sleep

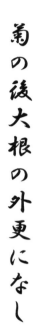

kiku no nochi
daikon no hoka
sara ni nashi

the chrysanthemums
done, not a thing will be left
but the radishes

158.

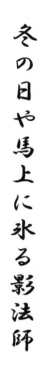

fuyu no hi ya
bajō ni kōru
kagebōshi

on a winter's day
on horseback, my shadow too
became frozen stiff

159.

旅に病で夢は枯野をかけ廻る

tabi ni yande
yume wa kareno o
kakemeguru

ill on a journey,
my dreams are wandering round
on a withered moor

160.

shira-uo ya
kuroki me o aku
nori no ami

whitebait, the small fry,
all open their jet black eyes
in the dharma's net

哀や歯に喰あてし海苔の砂

otoroi ya
ha ni kuiate shi
nori no suna

growing weak with age,
my teeth when i bite now grate
on sand in seaweed

162.

姥櫻さくや老後の思い出

uba-zakura
saku ya rōgo no
omoiide

**blooming in old age
are *old lady* cherry trees;
things to remember**

*30

世を旅にしろかく小田の行戻り

yo o tabi ni
shiro kaku oda no
yuki modori

the journey of life;
plowing a small field of rice
forwards and backwards

*31

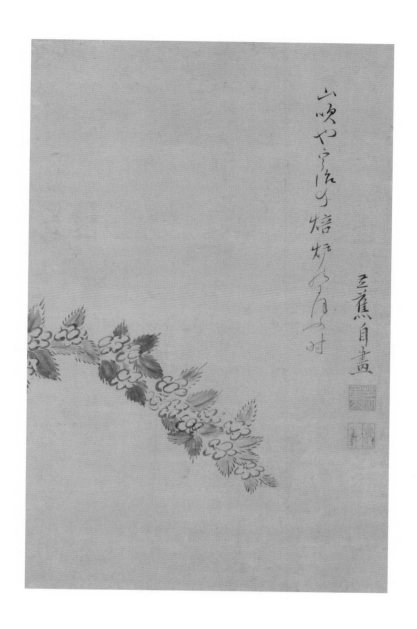

PLATE 9

Drawing and calligraphy by Basho,

Kakimori Bunko Foundation. See haiku 178.

193

164.

haru ya ko shi
toshi ya yuki ken
kotsugomori

**has the spring arrived
the year gone; it's december
twenty-ninth today**

165.

nani no ki no
hana to wa shirazu
nioi kana

what tree is in bloom
I really don't know at all;
yet the scent of it!

草臥て宿かる比や藤の花

kutabirete
yado karu koro ya
fuji no hana

being over-tired
looking for somewhere to stay;
the wisteria!

香にゝほへうにほる岡の梅のはな

ka ni nioe
uni horu oka no
ume no hana

the fragrant perfume
over the peat digging hill
is plum tree blossom

168.

蝶鳥のうはつきたつや花の雲

chō tori no
uwatsuki tatsu ya
hana no kumo

butterflies and birds
begin to get excited
in clouds of blossom

169.

uguisu ya
mochi ni fun suru
en no saki

a bush warbler left
its droppings on the rice-cakes
out on the platform

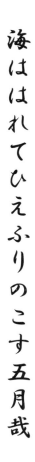

海ははれてひえふりのこす五月哉

umi wa harete
hie furi nokosu
satsuki kana

the lake has now cleared up
but there's rain on mount hiei;
the weather of may!

*32

171.

tsuru no ke no
kuroki koromo ya
hana no kumo

like a crane's feathers
your black robe as you go through
the clouds of blossom

172.

結ぶより早歯にひゞく泉かな

musubu yori
haya ha ni hibiku
izumi kana

as soon as i scooped
it up, my teeth were all shocked
by the spring water

173.

月ぞしるべこなたへ入せ旅の宿

tsuki zo shirube
konata e irase
tabi no yado

with the moon as a guide
please do come along this way
and enter our inn

*33

174.

観音のいらかみやりつ花の雲

kannon no
iraka miyari tsu
hana no kumo

the kannon temple's
tiled roof looks out over clouds
of cherry blossom

*34

175.

春の夜は櫻に明て仕廻けり

haru no yo wa
sakura ni akete
shimai keri

the spring night lit up
by dawn on the cherry trees
is brought to its end

176.

旅がらす古巣はむめに成にけり

tabigarasu
furu su wa mume ni
nari ni keri

a wandering crow
has found its old nest has turned
into plum blossom

177.

起よく我友にせんぬる胡蝶

okiyo okiyo
waga tomo ni sen
nuru kochō

wake up now, wake up now!
we will be good companions,
sleeping butterflies!

178.

山吹や宇治の焙炉の匂ふ時

yamabuki ya
uji no hoiro no
niou toki

yellow mountain rose!
the smell of uji green tea
comes from the drier

*35

物
好
や
匂
は
ぬ
草
に
と
ま
る
蝶

monozuki ya
niowa nu kusa ni
tomaru chō

a very strange whim;
although grass is not scented
butterflies visit

180.

うぐいすを魂にねむるか嬌柳

uguisu o
tama ni nemuru ka
tao yanagi

is the bush warbler
there, the soul of a sleeping,
graceful willow tree

181.

furu oto ya
mimi mo sūnaru
ume no ame

the sound of their fall
makes even my ears turn sour,
those plum tree raindrops

182.

hibari naku
naka no hyōshi ya
kiji no koe

amongst skylarks' songs
can be heard the rhythmical beat
of a pheasant's call

183.

shibashi ma mo
matsu ya hototogi
su sen nen

a short time to wait
for the first cuckoos' voices;
some thousands of years

PLATE 10
Drawing by Basho,
Kakimori Bunko Foundation.

184.

五月雨や桶の輪切る夜の声

samidare ya
oke no wa kiruru
yoru no koe

in the summer rain
the hoop of the pail has split,
a sound of the night

185.

子ども等よ昼顔咲キぬ瓜むかん

kodomora yo
hirugao saki nu
uri muka n

**children! the bindweed
flowers are blooming, i'll peel
a melon for you**

186.

samidare ya
shikishi hegi taru
kabe no ato

in the rains of may
the peeled-off poetry cards
leave marks on the wall

田一枚植て立去る柳かな

ta ichi mai
uete tachisaru
yanagi kana

after a whole patch
of paddy field had been sown
i left the willow

188.

蕣や是も又我が友ならず

*asagao ya
kore mo mata waga
tomo nara zu*

**the morning glories,
they also can never be
companions for me**

189.

玉祭けふも焼場のけぶり哉

tama matsuri
kyō mo yakiba no
keburi kana

the bon festival;
today too in the burning
ground the smoke goes up

*36

190.

家はみな杖にしら髪の墓参

ie wa mina
tsue ni shiraga no
haka-mairi

a whole family
with their sticks and their grey hairs
are visiting graves

191.

yorube o itsu
hito ha ni mushi no
tabine shite

when will it reach the shore,
that floating leaf; an insect
asleep on the trip

192.

おもしろうてやがてかなしき鵜舟哉

*omoshirō te
yagata kanashiki
ubune kana*

**how very exciting
the cormorant fishing boat,
but soon it was sad**

草
の
葉
を
落
る
よ
り
飛
螢
哉

kusa no ha o
otsuru yori tobu
hotaru kana

from a blade of grass
as it falls down, a firefly
is up and away

194.

夕顔にみとるゝや身もうかりひよん

yūgao ni
mitoruru ya mi mo
ukari hyon

bottle gourd blooms proved
so entrancing i was lost
in sheer wonderment

225

195.

馬ぼくく我をゑに見る夏野哉

uma boku boku
ware o e ni miru
natsuno kana

**a horse plodding slowly
through a summer field; it seems
a painting of me**

*37

196.

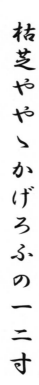

kare shiba ya
yaya kagerō no
ichi ni sun

over withered grass
just a little heat shimmer
for a few inches

PLATE 11
Drawing and calligraphy by Basho,
Tenri Central Library. See haiku 198.

228

197.

aki ki ni keri
mimi o tazunete
makura no kaze

now, the autumn has come,
a wind that blows over my
pillow to find my ear

198.

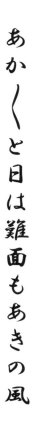

aka aka to
hi wa tsurenaku mo
aki no kaze

red, red is the sun,
relentless in its blazing;
the wind autumnal

199.

hyoro hyoro to
nao tsuyukeshi ya
ominaeshi

so slender, they seem
to be much more dewy still,
those maiden flowers!

200.

酔て寝むなでしこ咲ける石の上

yō te ne n
nadeshiko sake ru
ishi no ue

i wish i lay drunk
where the pinks are in flower
on top of the rocks

201.

蕎麦もみてけなりがらせよ野良の萩

soba mo mite
kenari gara seyo
nora no hagi

look at buckwheat too,
and make the field's bush clovers
envious of it

202.

秋涼し手毎にむけや瓜茄子

aki suzushi
te goto ni muke ya
uri nasubi

the autumn is cool,
let us peel with our own hands
egg plants and melons

203.

茸狩やあぶなきことに夕時雨

takegari ya
abunaki koto ni
yūshigure

hunting for mushrooms
and nearly caught by a cold
evening shower

204.

夕がおや秋はいろ／＼の瓢かな

yūgao ya
aki wa iroiro no
fukube kana

bottle gourd flowers
in autumn all turn into gourds
of different shapes

205.

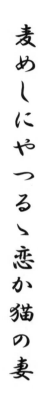

mugi meshi ni
yatsururu koi ka
neko no tsuma

boiled barley and love,
is that what caused such thinness
in a female cat

206.

けふの今宵寝る時もなき月見哉

kyō no koyoi
neru toki mo naki
tsukimi kana

**tonight's a special night
with no sleep at all because
of the moon-watching**

207.

名月や門に指くる潮頭

meigetsu ya
kado ni sashikuru
shio gashira

the harvest full moon,
coming right up to the gate,
the crest of full tide

208.

いなづまを手にとる闇の紙燭哉

inazuma o
te ni toru yami no
shisoku kana

you caught the lightning
in the darkness, it seems with
your paper candle

209.

庭掃て出ばや寺に散柳

niwa haite
ide baya tera ni
chiru yanagi

leaving the temple
i'd like to sweep the garden's
fallen willow leaves

210.

見送りのうしろや寂し秋の風

miokuri no
ushiro ya sabishi
aki no kaze

as i see you off
it is sad to see your back
in the autumn wind

211.

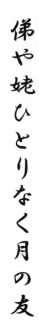

*omokage ya
oba hitori naku
tsuki no tomo*

**an old woman's face
alone and weeping, the moon
as her companion**

212.

武蔵野や一寸ほどな鹿の声

musashino ya
issun hodo na
shika no koe

on the grassy plain,
only about an inch high,
the call of a deer

*38

PLATE 12
Drawing by Basho,
Tenri Central Library.

213.

旅人と我名よばれん初しぐれ

tabibito to
waga na yoba re n
hatsushigure

traveller is what
i would like to be called in
the first winter rain

214.

月花もなくて酒のむひとり哉

tsuki hana mo
nakute sake nomu
hitori kana

without any moon
or flowers i'd have to drink
sake all alone

215.

乳麺の下たきたつる夜寒哉

nyūmen no
shita takitatsuru
yosamu kana

under boiled noodles
the fire is built up against
the cold of the night

216.

埋火や壁には客の影ぼうし

uzumibi ya
kabe ni wa kyaku no
kagebōshi

a banked charcoal fire
and on the wall can be seen
a guest's silhouette

217.

水仙や白き障子のとも移り

suisen ya
shiroki shōji no
tomo utsuri

narcissus flowers
and white paper screens are well
matched with each other

磨なをす鏡も清し雪の花

toginaosu
kagami mo kiyoshi
yuki no hana

now it is polished
the mirror is clear once more
to see snow petals

219.

煤掃は杉の木の間の嵐哉

susu haki wa
sugi no ko no ma no
arashi kana

soot cleaning this year
among japanese cedars,
a storm blowing through

*39

220.

toshi no ichi
senkō kai ni
ide baya na

the year's end market;
a few incense sticks are what
i'll go out and buy

221.

年暮ぬ笠きて草鞋はきながら

toshi kure nu
kasa kite waraji
haki nagara

another year gone
and my hat and straw sandals
are still being worn

PLATE 13
Drawing and calligraphy by Basho,
Tenri Central Library. See haiku 290.

255

222.

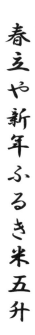

haru tatsu ya
shin-nen furuki
kome goshō

spring has just arrived;
for the new year i've five shō
of rice from last year

*40

223.

harusame ya
yomogi o nobasu
kusa no michi

the rain in the spring
makes the mugwort grow taller
in the grassy lane

224.

凍とけて筆に汲干ス清水哉

ite tokete
fude ni kumihosu
shimizu kana

as frozen ground thaws,
my brush is moistened enough
by the spring water

225.

ねぶかしろく洗あげたる寒さかな

nebuka shiroku
araiage taru
samusa kana

a white spring onion
after the washing is done,
how cold it appears

226.

此梅に牛も初音と啼つべし

kono ume ni
ushi mo hatsune to
naki tsu beshi

seeing plum blossom
the cow, at the year's first song,
must also have lowed

*41

227.

花をやどに
はじめをはりや
はつかほど

hana o yado ni
hajime owari ya
hatsuka hodo

making blossoms my inn
from start to finish, i stayed
about twenty days

馬に寝て残夢月遠し茶のけぶり

uma ni nete
zammu tsuki tōshi
cha no keburi

dozing on horseback
half dreaming, a faraway moon
and tea-making smoke

229.

散花や鳥もおどろく琴の塵

chiru hana ya
tori mo odoroku
koto no chiri

blossoms raining down,
birds surprised and dust moving
at the koto's sound

*42

230.

toshi doshi ya
sakura o koyasu
hana no chiri

year in and year out
the cherry trees are nourished
by fallen blossoms

231.

船足も休む時あり濱の桃

funaashi mo
yasumu toki ari
hama no momo

a boat sometimes seems
to lose headway and stand still;
peaches on the beach!

232.

花に酔り羽織着てかたな指す女

hana ni ee ri
haori kite katana
sasu onna

being drunk with blossoms,
a woman wearing a half coat
carrying a sword

233.

鸛の巣に嵐の外のさくら哉

kō no su ni
arashi no hoka no
sakura kana

a nest of white storks
was built out of a storm's reach
in a cherry tree

234.

うぐいすの笠おとしたる椿哉

uguisu no
kasa otoshi taru
tsubaki kana

a bush warbler
has allowed its hat to drop;
a camellia

235.

harusame ya
hachi no su tsutau
yane no mori

the rains of springtime
trickle on down a wasps' nest
through the leaking roof

236.

tsutsuji ikete
sono kage ni hidara
saku onna

potted azaleas,
and behind them a woman tears
up the dried codfish

237.

行春にわかの浦にて追付たり

yuku haru ni
wakanoura nite
oitsuki tari

with spring departing,
here at wakanoura
i have caught up with it

*43

271

238.

このほどを花に礼いふわかれ哉

kono hodo o
hana ni rei iu
wakare kana

for all these past days
i give thanks to the blossoms
and bid them farewell

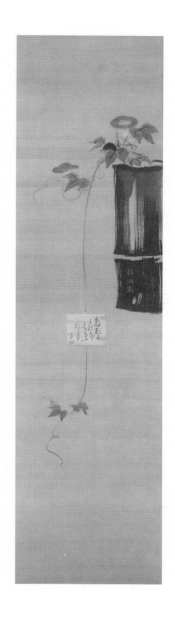

PLATE 14
Drawing by Icchō, calligraphy by Basho,
Tenri Central Library. See haiku 239.

239.

あさがほに我は食くふおとこ哉

asagao ni
ware wa meshi kū
otoko kana

**the morning glory
flowers make a good breakfast
for a man to eat**

kodai sasu
yanagi suzushi ya
ama ga tsuma

**skewering small sea
bream with cool twigs of willow,
a fisherman's wife**

241.

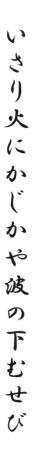

isaribi ni
kajika ya nami no
shita musebi

in the fishing light
a torrent frog sobs beneath
the waves, choked with tears

242.

世の人の見付ぬ花や軒の栗

yo no hito no
mitsuke nu hana ya
noki no kuri

people in this world
never notice the chestnut
blossom by the eaves

243.

karakasa ni
oshiwake mi taru
yanagi kana

with an umbrella
i have pushed through the branches
of the weeping willow

244.

taka no me mo
ima ya kure nu to
naku uzura

the eyes of the hawks
already dimmed by the dusk,
the quails are calling

245.

minazuki ya
tai wa are domo
shio-kujira

in the month of june
the sea bream are not as good
as the salted whale

246.

夏草や我先達で蛇からむ

natsukusa ya
waga sendachi de
hebi kara n

in the summer grass
i will gladly go ahead
to look out for snakes

247.

chō no ha no
ikutabi koyuru
hei no yane

a butterfly's wings,
how often is it they fly
over the roofed wall

248.

蛸壺やはかなき夢を夏の月

tako tsubo ya
hakanaki yume o
natsu no tsuki

an octopus pot
and ephemeral dreaming
in summer moonlight

*44

249.

tanoshisa ya
aota ni suzumu
mizu no oto

how blissful to cool
myself by the green rice fields,
hearing the water

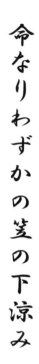

inochi nari
wazuka no kasa no
shita suzumi

it's a life saver
my small hat, underneath it
i enjoy some cool

251.

足洗てつる明安き丸寝かな

ashi arōte
tsui akeyasuki
marone kana

after washing my feet
with dawn on its way, i fell
asleep in my clothes

撞鐘もひゞくやうなり蟬の聲

tsuki gane mo
hibiku yō nari
semi no koe

the temple bell may
well start to reverberate
at cicadas' songs

253.

朝顔は下手のかくさへ哀也

asagao wa
heta no kaku sae
aware nari

a morning glory
even when badly painted
is still appealing

254.

夏の月御湯より出て赤坂か

natsu no tsuki
goyu yori idete
akasaka ya

the summer moon starts
at goyu and then ends up
at akasaka

*45

255.

いものはや月待さとの焼ばたけ

imo no ha ya
tsuki matsu sato no
yaki-batake

amid taro leaves
waiting for the harvest moon,
hamlet of burnt fields

*46

256.

meigetsu wa
futatsu sugite mo
seta no tsuki

the harvest moon seen
twice in one year, still passes
over seta bridge

*47

257.

飯あふぐかゝが馳走や夕涼

meshi aogu
kaka ga chisō ya
yū suzumi

a wife fans boiled rice,
the best dish for enjoying
the evening cool

258.

蛇くふときけばおそろし雉の声

hebi kuu to
kike ba osoroshi
kiji no koe

told that they eat snakes,
how dreadful it is to hear
a pheasant calling

259.

髪はえて容顔蒼し五月雨

kami haete
yōgan aoshi
satsuki ame

my hair has grown long
and my face is looking pale;
a long summer rain

260.

花にあそぶ虻なくらひそ友雀

hana ni asobu
abu na kurai so
tomo suzume

playing on flowers
there are horseflies; don't eat them
sparrows, they're your friends

261.

鼓子花の短夜ねぶる昼間哉

hirugao no
mijika yo neburu
hiruma kana

the bindweed flowers
look drowsy during the day
after a short night

262.

郭
公
声
横
た
ふ
や
水
の
上

hototogisu
koe yokotau ya
mizu no ue

the lesser cuckoo;
the sound of its voice still hangs
over the water

PLATE 15
Drawing by Icchō, calligraphy by Basho,
Tenri Central Library. See haiku 263.

263.

minomushi no
ne o kiki ni ko yo
kusa no io

come now and listen
to the sound the bagworms make
in my hermitage

264.

初秋や畳ながらの蚊屋の夜着

hatsu aki ya
tatami nagara no
kaya no yogi

in early autumn
a folded mosquito net
is my counterpane

265.

此秋は何で年よる雲に鳥

kono aki wa
nande toshi yoru
kumo ni tori

this autumn, why now
am i feeling old, a bird
flying into clouds

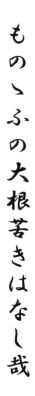

もののゝふの大根苦きはなし哉

mononofu no
daikon nigaki
hanashi kana

the samurai seemed
like a radish, so bitter
was the tale he told

267.

蕎麦はまだ花でもてなす山路かな

soba wa mada
hana de motenasu
yamaji kana

only buckwheat blooms
still for your entertainment
on a mountain road

榎の実ちるむくの羽音や朝あらし

e no mi chiru
muku no haoto ya
asa arashi

hackberries falling,
the sound of grey starlings' wings
is a morning storm

269.

荻の声こや秋風の口うつし

ogi no koe
koya akikaze no
kuchi utsushi

the voices of reeds
in the autumn wind become
like exact copies

270.

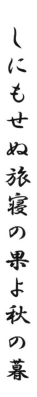

shini mo se nu
tabine no hate yo
aki no kure

not yet dead, asleep
at the end of a journey;
autumn evening

草枕犬も時雨〻かよるのこゑ

kusa-makura
inu mo shigururu ka
yoru no koe

at a poor lodging
with a dog that is whimpering
in the rain at night

272.

蚤虱馬の尿する枕もと

nomi shirami
uma no shito suru
makura-moto

the fleas and the lice,
and the horse passing water
next to my pillow!

273.

色付や豆腐に落て薄紅葉

irozuku ya
tōfu ni ochite
usu momiji

coloured maple leaves
falling down onto tofu
turn it slightly pink

*48

274.

名月に麓の霧や田のくもり

meigetsu ni
fumoto no kiri ya
ta no kumori

in the harvest moon,
fog at the foot of the hill,
mist on the paddies

275.

たびねして我句をしれや秋の風

tabine shite
waga ku o shire ya
aki no kaze

sleep on a journey
and you will know my haiku
in the autumn wind

276.

松風の落葉か水の音涼し

matsu kaze no
ochiba ka mizu no
oto suzushi

with wind in the pines
and needles falling, the sound
of water is cool

277.

秋風や藪も畠も不破の関

aki kaze ya
yabu mo hatake mo
fuwa no seki

the autumn winds blow
over bush and field where once
fuwa checkpoint stood

*49

278.

kiso no tochi
ukiyo no hito no
miyage kana

kiso horse chestnuts
in this ephemeral world
make good souvenirs

279.

木曽の瘦もまだなをらぬに後の月

kiso no yase mo
mada naora nu ni
nochi no tsuki

still thin from kiso
and not yet recovered,
i looked at the late moon

*51

280.

行雲や犬の尿むらしぐれ

yuku kumo ya
inu no kakebari
murashigure

from the scudding clouds
and a running dog pissing,
an autumn shower

281.

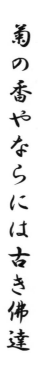

kiku no ka ya
nara ni wa furuki
hotoke tachi

**chrysanthemum scent
in nara among the wealth
of ancient buddhas**

*52

317

282.

蛤のふたみにわかれ行秋ぞ

hamaguri no
futami ni wakare
yuku aki zo

a clam from its shell,
i leave you for futami
as autumn departs

*53

283.

秋のいろぬかみそつぼもなかりけり

aki no iro
nukamiso tsubo mo
nakari keri

autumnal colours
and i haven't got even
one pickling jar left

284.

行秋や身に引まとふ三布蒲團

yuku aki ya
mi ni hikimatou
mino buton

autumn departing,
i pull the small cotton quilt
tighter and closer

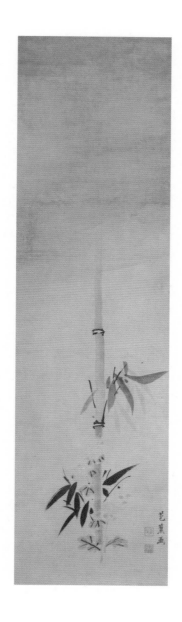

PLATE 16
Drawing by Basho,
Yamadera Basho Memorial Museum.

285.

omoshiroshi
yuki ni ya nara n
fuyu no ame

how interesting
that snow will soon be produced
out of winter rain

286.

初雪やいつ大仏の柱立

hatsu yuki ya
itsu daibutsu no
hashira date

the year's first snowfall;
when are daibutsu's columns
to be erected

*54

287.

貧山の釜霜に啼声寒し

hinzan no
kama shimo ni naku
koe samushi

at a poor temple
in frost, a weeping kettle
gives off a cold sound

湯の名残今宵は肌の寒からん

yu no nagori
koyoi wa hada no
samukara n

the hot spring water
will be missed tonight; the skin
will be feeling cold

かりて寝む案山子の袖や夜半の霜

karite ne n
kakashi no sode ya
yowa no shimo

**i'd like to borrow
a scarecrow's sleeves for sleeping
in the midnight frost**

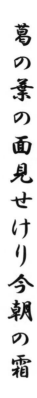

kuzu no ha no
omote mise keri
kesa no shimo

**the arrowroot leaves
have their faces all covered
in frost this morning**

291.

一露もこぼさぬ菊の氷かな

hito tsuyu mo
kobosa nu kiku no
kōri kana

not one drop of dew
is spilled by chrysanthemums'
ice covered flowers

292.

屏風には山を繪書て冬籠

byōbu ni wa
yama o egaite
fuyu-gomori

with a folding screen
that's depicting a mountain
he enjoys winter

もの一我がよはかろきひさご哉

mono hitotsu
waga yo wa karoki
hisago kana

owning but one thing,
my life in this world is light;
it's my gourd of rice

294.

米
買
に
雪
の
袋
や
投
頭
巾

kome kai ni
yuki no fukuro ya
nage zukin

**going to buy rice
in the snow, i used the bag
as a throw-back hood**

295.

花みなかれてあはれをこぼすくさのたね

hana mina karete
aware o kobosu
kusa no tane

the flowers all being dead,
how sad it is to see seeds
being shed by weeds

296.

石枯て水しぼめるや冬もなし

ishi karete
mizu shibomeru ya
fuyu mo nashi

the rocks are deadened
the water is all dried up;
a winter extreme

297.

kakure keri
shiwasu no umi no
kaitsuburi

now, hidden away
in the lake at the year's end
is a little grebe

298.

被き伏す鋪團や寒き夜やすごき

kazuki fusu
futon ya samuki
yo ya sugoki

**in bed with one's head
underneath the quilt, the cold
is dreadful at night**

299.

tsuki izuku
kane wa shizume ru
umi no soko

where now is the moon;
the temple bell is sunk down
to the sea bottom

300.

tsuki kage ya
shimon shishū mo
tada hitotsu

under the moonlight
the four gates and the four sects
are all of them one

*56

PLATE 17
Drawing by Basho,
Kakimori Bunko Foundation.

338

Notes

1. The bridge at Seta was a famous, major construction in the Chinese style, crossing the wide Seta River which flows down to the sea from Lake Biwa, the largest lake in Japan. In the lunar calendar early May sees the start of summer.

2. This would be summer in the lunar calendar.

3. *Shiogoshi*, or tide crossing, on the shore to the west of Kisagata in south-western Akita Prefecture, was a point at which an opening from the sea into a lagoon was passable at low tide. Kisagata, in the north-west of Honshu, the main island of Japan, was near the most northerly point reached by Basho in 1689. This was halfway through the most famous of his long journeys in search of poetic inspiration and was recorded by him in his main work *The Narrow Road to the Deep North* (*Oku no hosomichi*).

4. Suruga, one of the original Japanese provinces established in the Nara period, is now in Shizuoka Prefecture and bordered on the East by the Pacific coast some ninety miles south of Tokyo. Like Uji, it was famous for its fine tea, while the particular species of orange tree referred to bloomed in summer.

5. This refers, not to Basho's own hut, but to one built on a mountainside by a Chinese hermit monk, who lived in it for fifteen years, determined never to leave it before his death.

6. In the case of Basho's haiku, the Japanese word *hō* or *nori* has tradi-tionally always been translated as 'law', but is here rendered as 'dharma'. Following modern Buddhist conventions, the Three Treasures, *butsu*, *hō* and *sō* are translated as Buddha, Dharma and Sangha respectively, as people are nowadays familiar with the Sanskrit terms.

Morning glories flower in early July, which is the beginning of the seventh month in the solar calendar now in use, and therefore part of summer. In the lunar calendar, on the other hand, this, as it happens, comes at the end of the fifth month, which is also summer. Summer is therefore where we have placed morning glory flowers in this collec-tion of poems by Basho. However, in haiku they have traditionally been used as conventional markers for autumn, which may seem at first to be rather odd. However, this haiku may itself provide a clue as to the reason for this discrepancy, since it centres on the brevity of the lives both of monks and also of morning glories, the flowers of which are normally dead before autumn is over. If this is where the emphasis is placed, instead of on the beauty of the flowers in early summer, it may explain their particular use by Basho and those who followed him.

7. Sumadera, located in present-day Kobe, is an old Shingon Temple with connections to the conflicts between the Heike and the Genji clans. Kumagai Naozane, a famous Genji warrior, found himself forced to kill Taira no Atsumori, a young Heike samurai, on the coast of Suma in 1184. On discovering a flute played by the young man, Naozane realised who it was who had been playing such beautiful music at night during the conflict. Realising the impermanence of life, he became a devout disciple of Hōnen, the master of Shinran Shōnin, the founder of Shin Buddhism.

8. Minamidani temple, rebuilt a number of times, is only halfway up the 400 metre high Mount Haguro in Yamagata Prefecture in north-west Honshu, and since Basho climbed the mountain on the 3rd of June according to the lunar calendar and did not mention seeing snow when writing about it later, it is possible that the faint scent came from the nearly 2,000 metre high Mount Gassan known for its heavy snowfall.

9. For Mount Haguro, see above, note 8.

10. It may come as something of a surprise to those familiar with the haiku literature to find that Basho's poem referring to *arare*, translated as hailstones in this haiku, have been placed at the end of summer instead of in winter, but there are compelling historical and meteorological reasons for this. Neither Basho nor any of his fellow seventeenth century poets would have had any way of knowing how ice pellets or hailstones were actually formed or had reason to make seasonal distinctions between the two and the word *arare* covered both.

Ice pellets, with their irregular shape, indeed belong to cold, winter weather and come about when snow is partially melted on falling through a layer of warmer air, and then refrozen; whereas hailstones worldwide, which are normally spherical and formed by accretion, are a hot weather or summer phenomenon caused when the heated ground leads to the formation of cumulonimbus clouds in which supercooled droplets, initially carried on specks of pollen or dust, are repeatedly driven through sub-zero air by the violent updrafts and downdrafts until their increasing weight finally leads them to fall to earth.

11. With modern technology there are harvest seasons in summer and autumn, but in Basho's day there was only a late summer or autumn harvest so that in this case 'early' only refers to the first produce from the latter.

12. See above, note 11.

13. Sado is a large mountainous island, 31 miles off Niigata on the north-west coast of Honshu, and was well known in Basho's day for its association with Nichiren Shōnin (1222–1282), the founder of the Buddhist sect named after him.

14. Mount Hira (4,000 ft) and the lower Mount Mikami (1,417 ft) are mountains flanking the southern end of Lake Biwa.

15. Ōtsu-e, in Japanese, was the name given to the folk art sold to pilgrims passing through Otsu, the main port on Lake Biwa in order to visit Miidera Temple at the foot of Mount Hiei, the great Tendai Buddhist centre where Shinran Shōnin (1173–1263) had begun his studies.

16. Pounding rice cakes is normally done in the winter, as shown in haiku 71, but in this case pounding refers to the removal of the bran which is done at any time.

17. The Ueno referred to was not Iga-Ueno, near Kyoto, where Basho was born, but the district in Edo which is now, like nearby Asakusa, part of the vastly expanded modern city renamed Tokyo at the time of the Meiji Restoration in 1868.

18. In Pure Land Buddhism, the *nenbutsu* is the expression of joy and gratitude for all that Amida Buddha has, in his infinite compassion, done for them, and opens the gate to the Pure Land which is their ultimate goal in life.

19. Urami Falls, about four miles west of Nikko in the mountains north of Tokyo, were notable for having a cave behind the main waterfall, now inaccessible because of a 1905 earthquake, in which Basho proposed to stay to view the fall and begin the ninety day period of seclusion prescribed for Buddhist monks each summer.

20. The Saga referred to, where Basho stayed in a villa owned by his disciple, Kyorai, for 17 days in the summer of 1691, was at that time an area a short distance from Kyoto, by which it was subsequently engulfed. While there, he wrote his only diary and in it refers to the surrounding bamboo groves, a spectacular example of which still survives in nearby Arashiyama, now in Kyoto.

21. The Mogami is a major, fast flowing river running down through Yamagata to reach the Japan Sea at Sakata.

22. Oku is an abbreviation of Ōshū (or Mutsu) Province in northern Honshu. His time there is recorded in Basho's main work, *The Narrow Road to the Deep North* (*Oku no hosomichi*).

23. This lament is for Isshō, a famous poet in Kanazawa on the west coast of Honshu, of whom Basho had heard. The latter's brother told him that his fellow poet was anxiously hoping to meet him, but unfortunately when Basho reached Kanazawa in July in the course of his most famous journey, he was told, to his great dismay, that Isshō had died.

24. The word 'tomb' does not occur in Basho's haiku, but is frequently added in English translations, since the poem refers to Minamoto no Tomonaga who was taken seriously ill after being wounded in Kyoto and repeated the *nenbutsu* twice before committing suicide.

25. This lament was when Basho returned home long after his mother's death and his elder brother showed him an amulet containing a lock of her white hair.

26. A fulling block was a piece of wood used for beating cloth by hand to soften or extend it.

27. As is mentioned in the Introduction (p. 17) in relation to apparent synaesthesia, the reference to 'calls' becoming faintly white may go back to the Taoist system of correspondences in which white was the colour of autumn.

28. Stone Mountain refers to a rock at Nata-dera, a Shingon temple, which was built on a hill, known for its white quartzite, in Kaga Province, facing the Sea of Japan, which Basho visited in his journey to Ōshū.

29. For the use of the word 'dharma', see above, note 6.

30. *Old Lady* cherry trees are remarkable for blooming without leaves and were therefore associated with the idea of becoming old and toothless. In the lunar calendar this would belong to spring, but it has been placed where it is because its content goes so well with the theme of old age in the preceding poem.

31. Because it is a summary of Basho's whole life, this haiku has been placed here rather than in its lunar calendar position in summer. It is, however, interesting from the western point of view to note that in the succeeding haiku, no. 164, Basho apparently makes use of another solar system calendar, known as "The 24 divisions of the Solar Year", which was developed in China in ancient times and later brought to Japan together with Chinese literature.

32. Mt. Hiei, some 10 miles north-east of Kyoto, became, from a starting point in the late eighth century, the increasingly powerful headquarters of Tendai Buddhism. Shinran Shōnin (1173–1263) and Nichiren Shōnin (1222–1292) both studied there before the latter went on to develop the particular forms of Buddhist practice and belief associated with his name. In the lunar calendar this would refer to summer.

33. Although the moon is usually seen as autumnal through its association with the harvest full moon there is no good reason for seeing an innkeeper's plea as being restricted in this way.

34. The Kannon temple, or Sensōji, in Asakusa, now part of Tokyo, is named in honour of Bodhisattva Kannon (Avalokiteśvara in Sanskrit), known as the Goddess of Mercy. The temple complex includes the Asakusa Shinto shrine, the largest in Tokyo.

35. Uji, a small town between Kyoto and Nara, was famous, among other things, for its production of especially fine green tea.

36. The Bon Festival in honour of the ancestral spirits, who return for a short time, is still held in July or August in Japan. In Basho's day it would be held in autumn on the fifteenth of the seventh month in the lunar calendar.

37. This haiku was inspired by a painting which Basho saw when he was staying with Takayama Biji, a chief retainer of the Akimoto clan, after the small rustic house built for him by a disciple in Fukagawa outside Edo, now Tokyo, was destroyed by a conflagration in December 1682.

38. Musashino, though now a part of Tokyo was, in the preceding Edo period, the name of a vast grassy plain, celebrated in poetry throughout the recorded history of Japan as the paradigm of wide open spaces. The relationship to synaesthesia is considered in the Introduction (p. 17).

39. This poem is a transposition of the annual house cleaning, especially involving the clearing of soot from walls and ceilings with bamboo branches, which took place annually on December 13th in preparation for the New Year Festival.

40. A *shō* was a traditional measure amounting to about 1.8 litres, and Basho had a large gourd with a nine litre capacity which his disciples topped up with rice, and which he referred to elsewhere as his sole possession.

41. The cow referred to is one of the images associated with the many Shinto shrines dedicated to Tenjin, the kami of scholarship and learning, the cow being venerated as his divine messenger.

42. The *koto*, which has become the national instrument of Japan, is a horizontal board instrument very slightly raised above the floor and having thirteen silk strings and movable bridges. Its European counterpart is the usually much less elegant zither.

43. Wakanoura, famous for the natural beauty of its surroundings and some sixty miles or so from Nara, was about the most southerly point that he reached on the eleven month journey begun near the end of 1687, which he recorded in *The Records of a Travel-Worn Satchel* (*Oi no kobumi*).

44. This concerns an octopus holed up in one of the sunken earthenware pots which were used as a form of trap.

45. Goyu and Akasaka are now two districts subsumed in modern Tokyo and are actually only about a mile apart.

46. Taro, with its edible leaves and base of stem, was grown on land cultivated by the ancient slash and burn method and was an important food at the time of the August 15th Harvest Moon Festival.

47. In 1691 in the lunar calendar August occurred twice in order to regularise it, and the moon therefore passed twice over the great bridge across the wide Seta river.

48. Tofu, or bean curd, is made by coagulating fresh soy milk and then pressing the resulting curds into soft white blocks.

49. This is a reference to one of the innumerable barriers maintained by the Tokugawa regime on the often wild and dangerous highways of Basho's day in order to maintain political control, check on documents, catch criminals and others considered to be undesirable by the authorities, and to control the flow of goods. Basho, though not a monk, sometimes shaved his head and wore monks' robes to make it easier to pass through such checkpoints.

50. Kiso was a very small town in the district of the same name in Nagano Prefecture skirting the Central Alps north-west of Tokyo. The Kiso valley, along which ran the Nakasendō highway connecting Edo, as Tokyo then was, with Kyoto, was noted for its scenic quality.

51. The 'late moon' was the bright moon occurring on September 13th according to the lunar calendar.

52. The many temples in Nara, the first major capital of Japan, housed numerous Buddha figures other than the famous giant Buddha in Todaiji.

53. The reference to Futami, not far from the great Shinto shrine at Ise, occurs in the last poem that he wrote towards the end of his most famous, six month long journey. This finished in Ogaki, some 25 miles north-west of Nagoya, and was recorded in *The Narrow Road to Oku* (*Oku no hosomichi*, 1689), one of the best known texts in Japanese classical literature.

54. The rebuilding of the great hall housing Daibutsu, the 15 metre high bronze Buddha of Todaiji in Nara, was completed in 1709 and though on a smaller scale than the original is still the largest such structure ever built.

55. In the course of his travels Basho had been impressed by an inn-keeper's evocative story of a temple bell that had fallen into the sea, but could not be raised because it was upside down and divers had been unable to reach its dragon-headed eye to attach a rope.

56. This haiku refers to Zenkōji in Nagano, 240 miles north-west of Tokyo, which was founded in the seventh century and came to be run by the Tendai and Jōdoshū schools, associated with Shinshū, Jishū and other Buddhist sects. It has been set here as the final haiku in this selection since it epitomises the entirely non-sectarian nature of Basho's approach to Buddhism.

Index of First Lines and Illustrations

PLATE 2

hatsu makuwa	the year's first melon;	16
samidare ni	heavy summer rain	17
shiogoshi ya	crossing at low tide	18
sazaregani	a very small crab	19
hara-naka ya	out over the plain	20
ayame-gusa	irises, it seems,	21
surugaji ya	on the suruga	22
shizukasa ya	amid the stillness	23
kitsutsuki mo	even woodpeckers	24
kozue yori	out of a treetop	25
sō asagao	monks and morning glories,	26
yagate shinu	they will die so soon,	27
natsukusa ya	the summer grasses;	28
mizuumi ya	high over the lake	29
sumadera ya	in sumadera	30
arigata ya	how grateful i am	31
suzushiza ya	what coolness; a faint	32
hototogisu	a cuckoo calling;	33
suzushisa o	making the coolness	34
chimaki yuu	wrapping rice dumplings,	35
michinobe no	there by the roadside	36
no o yoko ni	crossing the moorland	37
magusa ou	people with fodder	38
yami no yo ya	in the night's darkness	39
ikameshiki	how harsh is the sound	40

PLATE 3

inazuma ya	a flash of lightning!	41
kono michi ya	along this pathway	42
nozarashi o	resigned to dying	43
kari ato ya	in harvested fields	44
inoshishi no	a wild boar it seems	45

akebono ya	in morning half-light	46
kiku no hana	chrysanthemums bloom	47
bashō-ba o	let's hang banana	48
meigetsu no	under the full moon	49
yoki ie ya	a very nice house;	50
ina-suzume	for rice-field sparrows	51
kusa no to o	at the grassy gate	52
ushibeya ni	in the cattle shed,	53
nami no ma ya	in between the waves	54
ama no ya wa	a fisherman's hut;	55
mi ni shimite	the bitter radish	56
bashō nowaki shite	banana tree in autumn storm,	57
wase no ka ya	an early rice smell	58
shizu no ko ya	a peasant's young child	59
araumi ya	tempestuous sea;	60
hira mikami	hira, mikami;	61
kare-eda ni	on a tree's dead branch	62

PLATE 4

shigure o ya	a winter shower	63
fuyugare ya	winter withering,	64
kame waruru	a water jar burst	65
robiraki ya	fireplace opening;	66
shiore fusu ya	being bowed down so low,	67
kogarashi ya	the cold winter winds	68
kimi hi take	if you light a fire	69
akebono ya	in the dawn's half-light	70
ariake mo	a pale morning moon	71

PLATE 5

haru mo yaya	now the springtime scene	72
niwa hakite	sweeping the garden,	73
ōtsu-e no	painters in otsu	74

furudera no	at an old temple	75
utagau na	have no doubts at all;	76
kashi no ki no	the evergreen oak	77
saki midasu	peaches in full bloom	78
yoku mireba	if you look with care,	79
uguisu ya	a bush warbler there	80
hana no kumo	cherry blossom clouds;	81
yo ni sakaru	cherries in blossom;	82
shibaraku wa	for a little while	83
ki no moto ni	underneath the tree	84
hana ni nenu	looking at blossoms	85
yuku haru ya	spring is departing	86

PLATE 6

shibaraku wa	shut for a short while	87
hitotsu nuide	taking one garment off	88
chichi haha no	father and mother,	89
kirisame no	with a misty rain	90
hototogisu	the lesser cuckoo	91
takenoko ya	a bamboo shoot, when	92
suzume-go to	the baby sparrows	93
waga yado wa	in my dwelling place	94
hana wa shizu no	for all the poor people	95
kogakurete	hidden by bushes	96
kane kiete	the bell's sound dies down,	97
sara bachi mo	the plates and the bowls	98
furusu tada	only an old nest,	99
ki o kirite	the cleanly sawn end	100
kumo ori ori	once in a while a cloud	101
yama mo niwa mo	the garden and mountains	102
hiya hiya to	i feel the coolness	103
tonbō ya	a dragonfly tried	104
suzushisa o	the coolness itself	105
ran no ka ya	a scented orchid	106

yūbe ni mo	it is not confined	107
atsuki hi o	it sweeps the burning	108
hotaru mi ya	out firefly viewing	109
hototogisu	the lesser cuckoo,	110
fūryū no	it seems elegance	111
furazu tomo	even with no rain	112
sazanami ya	among rippling waves	113
samidare ni	in this summer rain	114
kono hotaru	i like to compare	115
hiru mire ba	by the light of day	116
kuwa no mi ya	the mulberry fruit	117

PLATE 7

tsuka mo ugoke	move, oh burial mound!	118
muzan ya na	how woeful it is;	119
koke uzumu	out of the mosses	120
te ni toraba kien	were i to take it in my hand	121
inazuma ni	seeing the lightning	122
kumo nan to	spider, with what voice	123
asa na asa na	morning in, morning out,	124
koe sumite	clear, echoing sound	125
tsuyu toku toku	the drip, drip of the dew	126
kakehashi ya	on the hanging bridge,	127
hōzuki wa	the lantern plant's leaves	128
rusu no ma ni	all is deserted	129
momotose no	a century old	130
hitotsu ya ni	under the same roof	131
ika uri no	cuttlefish sellers'	132
tsuru naku ya	the screech of a crane	133
inoshishi mo	even the wild boars	134
kari kake shi	with harvest starting,	135
meigetsu ya	an autumn full moon;	136
kiku no ka ya	chrysanthemum scent;	137
sato furite	the hamlet is old,	138

ka ni nioe	the fragrant perfume	167
chō tori no	butterflies and birds	168
uguisu ya	a bush warbler left	169
umi wa harete	the lake has now cleared up	170
tsuru no ke no	like a crane's feathers	171
musubu yori	as soon as i scooped	172
tsuki zo shirube	with the moon as a guide	173
kannon no	the kannon temple's	174
haru no yo wa	the spring night lit up	175
tabigarasu	a wandering crow	176
okiyo okiyo	wake up now, wake up now!	177
yamabuki ya	yellow mountain rose!	178
monozuki ya	a very strange whim;	179
uguisu o	is the bush warbler	180
furu oto ya	the sound of their fall	181
hibari naku	amongst skylarks' songs	182
shibashi ma mo	a short time to wait	183

PLATE 10

samidare ya	in the summer rain	184
kodomora yo	children! the bindweed	185
samidare ya	in the rains of may	186
ta ichi mai	after a whole patch	187
asagao ya	the morning glories,	188
tama matsuri	the bon festival;	189
ie wa mina	a whole family	190
yorube o itsu	when will it reach the shore,	191
omoshirō te	how very exciting	192
kusa no ha o	from a blade of grass	193
yūgao ni	bottle gourd blooms proved	194
uma boku boku	a horse plodding slowly	195
kare shiba ya	over withered grass	196

PLATE 11

PLATE 12

PLATE 13

meigetsu wa	the harvest moon seen	256
meshi aogu	a wife fans boiled rice,	257
hebi kuu to	told that they eat snakes,	258
kami haete	my hair has grown long	259
hana ni asobu	playing on flowers	260
hirugao no	the bindweed flowers	261
hototogisu	the lesser cuckoo;	262

PLATE 15

minomushi no	come now and listen	263
hatsu aki ya	in early autumn	264
kono aki wa	this autumn, why now	265
mononofu no	the samurai seemed	266
soba wa mada	only buckwheat blooms	267
e no mi chiru	hackberries falling,	268
ogi no koe	the voices of reeds	269
shini mo se nu	not yet dead, asleep	270
kusa-makura	at a poor lodging	271
nomi shirami	the fleas and the lice,	272
irozuku ya	coloured maple leaves	273
meigetsu ni	in the harvest moon,	274
tabine shite	sleep on a journey	275
matsu kaze no	with wind in the pines	276
aki kaze ya	the autumn winds blow	277
kiso no tochi	kiso horse chestnuts	278
kiso no yase mo	still thin from kiso	279
yuku kumo ya	from the scudding clouds	280
kiku no ka ya	chrysanthemum scent	281
hamaguri no	a clam from its shell,	282
aki no iro	autumnal colours	283
yuku aki ya	autumn departing,	284

PLATE 16

PLATE 17